CALGARY PUBLIC LIBRARY

AUG - 2012

D1165009

BRUCE GOLDSTONE

AWESOME AUTUMN

HENRY HOLT AND COMPANY

NEW YORK

AUTUMN IS A SEASON OF AWESOME CHANGES.

Look around in autumn and you'll see a lot of changes happening. These changes take plants, animals, and people from the hot days of summer to the cold days of winter.

DAYS GET COLDER...

At the beginning of autumn,
you might be comfortable running
around in a T-shirt and shorts.

. . . SO YOUR CLOTHES GET
HEAVIER.

By the end of autumn, you're more likely to be wearing a sweater, long pants, and a jacket.

DAYS GET SHORTER...

Autumn begins on the autumnal equinox. In the Northern Hemisphere, that's a day near September 22 when day and night are both 12 hours long.

...AND NIGHTS GET LONGER.

Autumn ends on the winter solstice.
In the Northern Hemisphere, that's a
day near December 22. It's the shortest
day of the year.

LEAVES CHANGE COLOR.

WHY DO LEAVES CHANGE?

To understand the answer, you need to know why leaves are green in spring and summer.

The green color in a leaf comes from chlorophyll (KLOR-uh-fill). Unlike you, plants make their own food, and they use chlorophyll to do it. This green chemical traps energy from sunlight. Plants use the energy to grow.

Summer days are long and bright, so leaves have plenty of light to make food.

In autumn, days get shorter. Many plants stop making food when daylight decreases.

As days get shorter, leaves stop producing chlorophyll. The trees don't need it anymore. When the chlorophyll is gone, we can see new colors in the leaves.

THOSE ARE THE COLORS OF AUTUMN.

ANOTHER NAME FOR AUTUMN IS FALL.

BUT HOW DO LEAVES KNOW WHEN IT'S TIME TO FALL?

Some trees have leaves that can't survive in winter. Their branches and trunks are strong enough to live through the cold, short days ahead. But their thin green leaves are too delicate and would die in the cold. That's why these trees drop them.

Leaves have veins that carry fluids in and out of the leaf. As autumn days get shorter, the veins begin to close off. Fluids stop moving in and out. A layer forms at the base of each leaf where it hangs on the tree. Finally, this layer completely seals off the leaf from the tree. When the leaf is no longer connected to the living part of the tree, it can fall.

Trees that drop their leaves in autumn are called deciduous trees.

WHAT HAPPENS TO ALL THOSE LEAVES?

Leaves that fall can help keep the environment healthy. As they break down, they give food to the earth and to tiny living things in the soil. Fallen leaves also act as sponges. They mix with the soil to help it hold rainwater.

WHAT TREES DID THESE LEAVES COME FROM?

beech

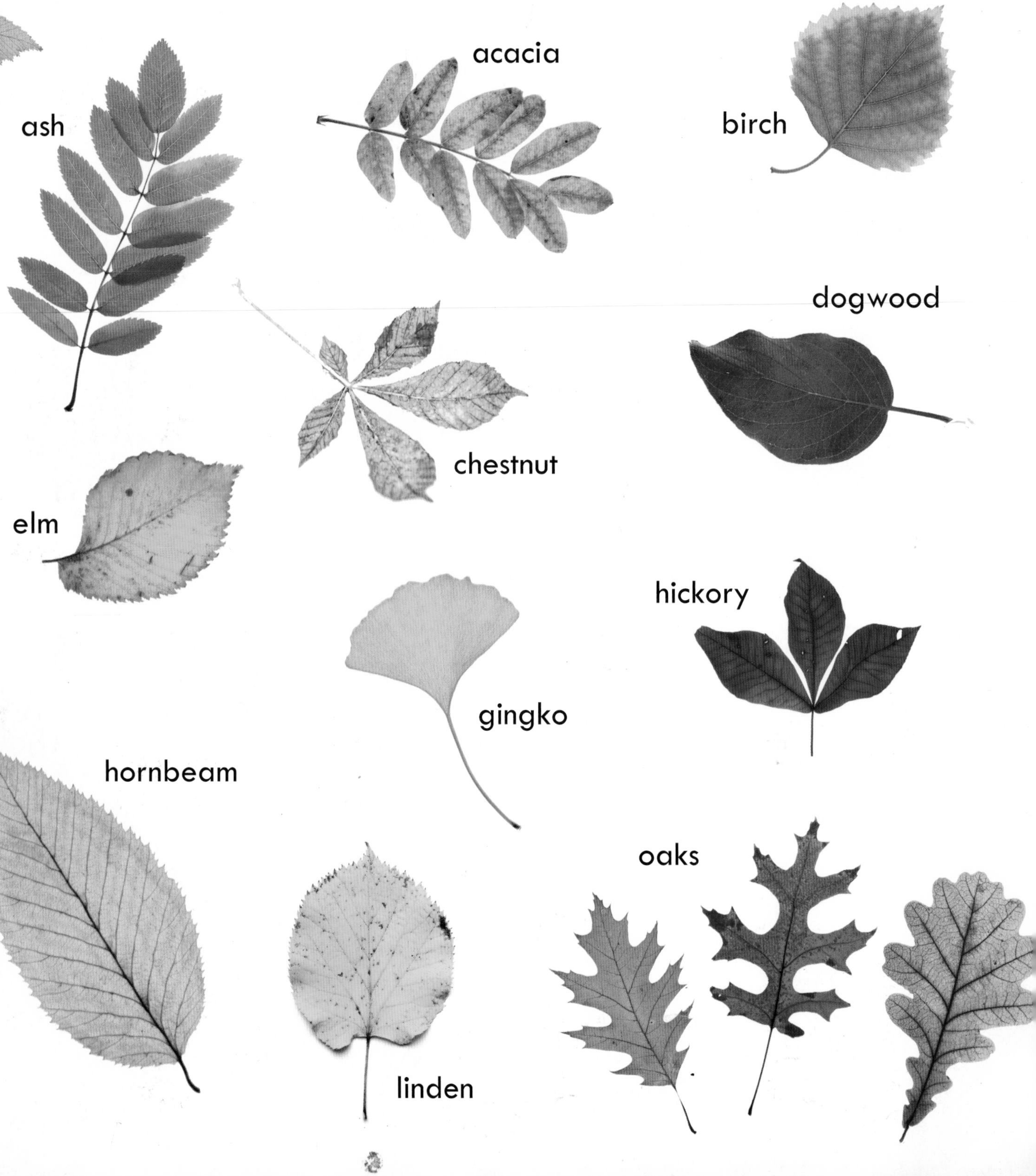

acacia

ash

birch

dogwood

chestnut

elm

hickory

gingko

hornbeam

oaks

linden

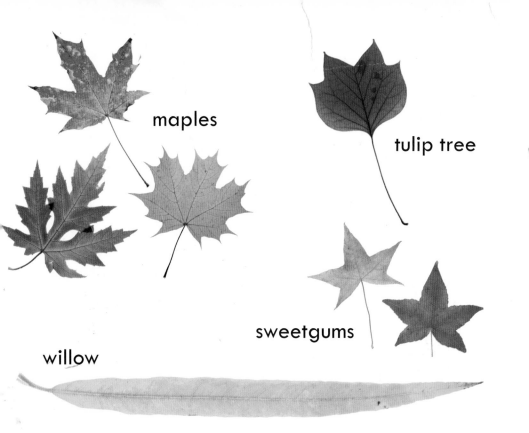
maples

tulip tree

sassafras
(3 different leaf shapes
found on the same tree!)

sweetgums

willow

WHAT ELSE FALLS TO THE GROUND?

acorns

plane tree nuts

maple seeds

osage oranges
(monkey brains)

chinese
lanterns

horse chestnuts
(buckeyes)

pine
cones

honey locust
seed pods

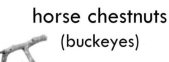

HOW DOES AUTUMN FEEL?

fluffy

bumpy

smooth

icy

slimy

spiky

slippery

crispy

soft

warm

hard

NOT EVERYTHING CHANGES IN AUTUMN.

pine

spruce

EVERGREENS STAY
EVER GREEN.

Evergreens are tough enough to stay green all winter. Their needles or leaves are covered with a heavy wax that helps them survive in the winter. This wax keeps the moisture in an evergreen from freezing.

hemlock

holly

fir

cedar

AUTUMN
BRINGS
FROST.

HOW DOES
FROST FORM?

Frost is frozen dew. But what's dew?

Air looks invisible, but it isn't empty.
Air always has some moisture in it.
The air close to the ground gets moisture
from soil and plants. During cool nights,
the moisture in the air also cools. Moisture
becomes droplets on plants, the ground,
and even spiderwebs. These drops are dew.

In autumn, nighttime temperatures can
drop below the freezing point. Moisture
in the air freezes into ice crystals. That's
frost, and it can mean trouble for plants.
When the temperature is cold enough to
form frost, water inside the plant freezes,
too. As a result, the plant may die.

BEFORE THE FROST COMES, IT'S **TIME TO HARVEST CROPS.**

FARMERS USE EVERYTHING FROM THEIR HANDS TO MIGHTY MACHINES.

Some crops are best harvested by hand to make sure they don't get bruised.

Other crops are best harvested by machine. A combine is used to harvest grains like wheat, barley, rye, and corn. The name comes from the fact that it combines three different jobs: cutting, threshing, and cleaning. First, the machine pushes stalks of grain into the correct position and cuts them. Next, a conveyor carries the grain into the threshing drum. That's where the chaff—the outer part of the grain that can't be eaten—is removed. Finally, the grain is cleaned and then transferred to a truck that carries it to be milled.

HOW DOES AUTUMN TASTE?

Lots of crops are ripe and ready to eat in the fall.

Apples, pumpkins, pears, plums, and more!

A cornucopia is a horn of plenty. It's filled with fruits, nuts, and vegetables that you can taste in autumn.

WHAT SHAPE IS AUTUMN?

Look for shapes in autumn. What do you see that's round?

What do you see that's shaped like a triangle or an eye?

HOW DOES AUTUMN SOUND?

BOO!
spooky nights

MMMM!
munching tasty fall treats

HONK!
geese on the go

CRINKLE!
leaves under your feet

SWOOSH!
wind in trees

HOORAY!

fans at a football game

THWACK!

combine cutting wheat

HISS!

black Halloween cat

GOBBLE!

Thanksgiving turkey

IN AUTUMN, SOME BIRDS
LEAVE TOWN.

Many birds migrate—they fly south to spend the winter where it is warmer and food is more plentiful. You might see geese or other birds flying in a V. This pattern saves energy. The bird in front works the hardest, cutting through the air's resistance. The air behind the front bird has a little less resistance, so it's easier to fly through. Birds take turns flying in front.

Here are some birds that migrate.

duck

swans

goose

pelican

egret

arctic tern

The tiny arctic tern has the longest migration of any animal. Every year, this 4-ounce bird flies more than 44,000 miles from Greenland to Antarctica and back again!

MIGRATING ISN'T JUST FOR BIRDS.

Ocean waters get colder in the autumn. Dolphins and whales also migrate, following warmer water currents.

SOME INSECTS MIGRATE, TOO.

Monarch butterflies, grasshoppers, and some dragonflies travel hundreds or even thousands of miles to reach their winter homes.

SOME ANIMALS DON'T MIGRATE SOUTH; THEY MIGRATE DOWN.

Mountain goats, bighorn sheep, and elk that live high in the mountains during the summer move down to lower, warmer lands in the autumn.

SOME ANIMALS DON'T MOVE IN AUTUMN. INSTEAD, THEY STOP MOVING.

Many animals become much less active in the late fall. Chipmunks, hedgehogs, bats, frogs, toads, and even earthworms hibernate. They seem to be sleeping for a very, very long time. Their body temperature and heartbeat decrease. They live off fat stored in their body.

Bears spend the cold season in caves, hollow trees, or dens. They can sleep for as long as a month. But they can also wake up if they are threatened. Before they go to sleep, bears prepare their sleeping areas by lining them with dried leaves and grasses. These materials help to keep out the cold.

ANIMALS WHO STAY AWAKE IN THE WINTER USE AUTUMN DAYS TO GET READY FOR THE COLD.

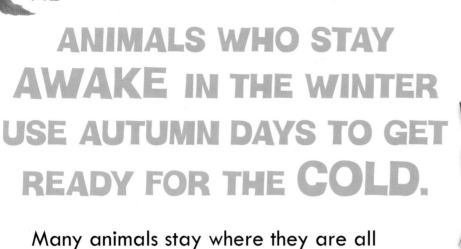

Many animals stay where they are all year round. In the autumn, they gather food while it is plentiful. Squirrels, beavers, and other mammals store food for the winter. Some mammals like foxes grow thicker fur in the autumn. This helps them stay warm as temperatures drop.

Summer   Winter

Other mammals like
the snowshoe hare and the
ermine even change colors.
Their fur changes from brown
to white to blend in better
with the winter snow.

Summer   Winter

WHAT DO PEOPLE DO IN AUTUMN?

Rake leaves into a pile. Then jump!

Play soccer and football.

People still play baseball in autumn, too. The World Series ends baseball season in October.

WHAT WILL YOU BE ON HALLOWEEN?

Halloween comes every October 31. It began as a holiday to bridge the light part of the year and the dark part. People wore masks and costumes to scare away spirits from the dark world.

Today, many kids wear costumes to go trick-or-treating. Some costumes are scary, others are silly. When you put on a costume, you get to pretend you are someone—or something—else for a little while.

green beans

stuffing

WHAT FOOD WILL YOU SHARE ON THANKSGIVING?

pecan pie

Thanksgiving started as a harvest festival. Families gather together to show they are thankful for the food of the growing season.

Thanksgiving traditions go back to 1621. The Pilgrims of the Plymouth Colony wanted to celebrate their first successful harvest in a new country. The Wampanoag, an eastern Native American tribe, joined the festivities, which lasted three days.

cranberry sauce

sweet corn

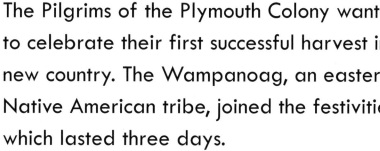
gravy

turkey

Brussels sprouts

pumpkin pie

yams

mashed potatoes

People in the United States celebrate Thanksgiving on the fourth Thursday in November. In Canada, Thanksgiving comes on the second Monday in October.

FINALLY,
THE LAST
CHANGE OF
AUTUMN
ARRIVES.

AWESOME AUTUMN TURNS INTO
WONDERFUL WINTER.

Soon, the cool of fall turns into the cold of winter. Tree branches are bare. A blanket of fresh snow might cover the leaves on the ground. What other changes will winter bring?

SOME AWESOME AUTUMN ACTIVITIES

leaf
rubbings

pressed leaves

roasted pumpkin seeds

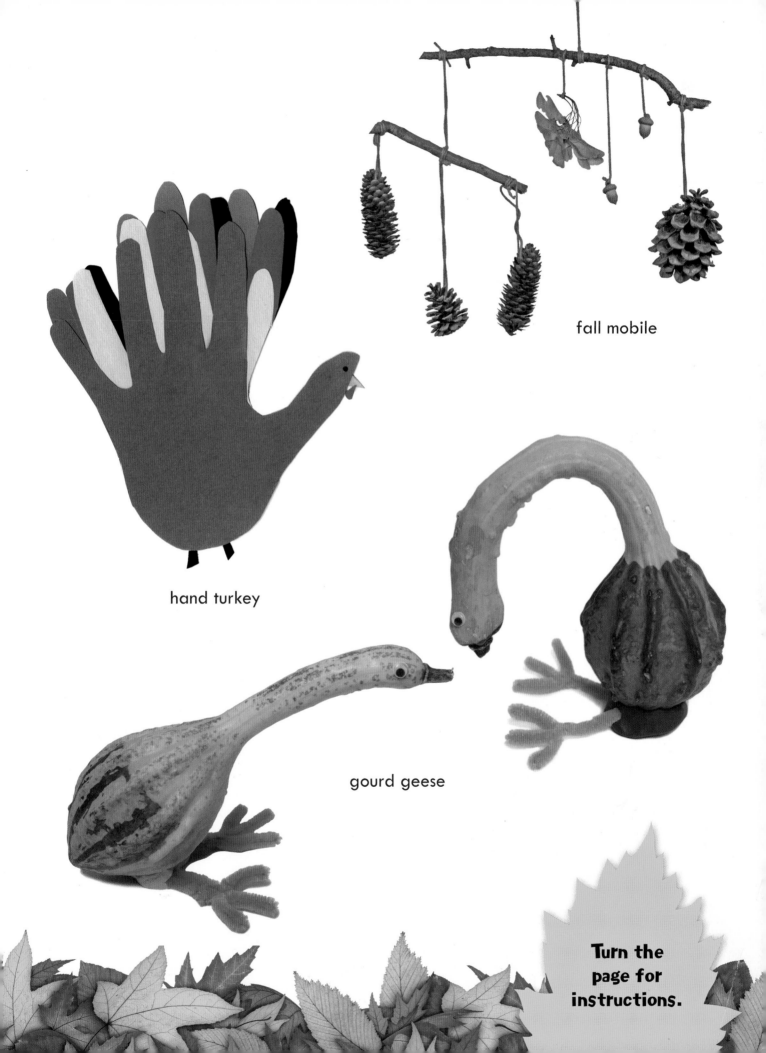

fall mobile

hand turkey

gourd geese

Turn the page for instructions.

PRESSED LEAVES

Here are two ways you can press the colorful leaves you find in the fall. Choose leaves that are as flat as possible.

WAX PAPER METHOD: Cover your ironing board with an old towel or cloth. Place a sheet of wax paper on the towel. Arrange one layer of leaves on the wax paper and cover it with another piece of wax paper. Then cover the wax papers with another towel. (The towels keep the wax from harming your iron or board.) Have an adult press the leaves with an iron using high heat, but no steam. Apply light pressure at first. Once the wax paper begins to stick, press a bit harder for about 5 seconds on each area. Allow to cool. If you want, you can cut out the leaves. Allow a small edge around each leaf to keep the wax paper sealed.

WEIGHT METHOD: Place leaves between sheets of newspaper or wax paper. Place the paper inside the pages of a heavy book. Add weight by stacking more books on top. Check leaves after one week. Most leaves take at least three weeks to dry. (Variation: If you want to end up with a leaf that is dry but more flexible, soak it in a mixture of fabric softener and water before you place it between wax paper sheets.)

GOURD GOOSE

Place some modeling clay on the bottom of a gourd so it sits up. Bend feet out of pipe cleaners and stick them into the clay. Glue on googly eyes.

HAND TURKEY

Trace your hand several times on different colored construction paper. Cut out the hands (use safety scissors or ask an adult for help). Cut the thumb off all but one hand—that's your turkey body. Fan out the rest of the hands behind the turkey body and glue them together to create feathers. Cut out legs, a yellow beak, and a red wattle (that's the wobbly thing under the beak) and glue them onto the body. Add an eye with a marker or a construction paper dot.

FALL MOBILE

Use yarn to tie your fall collection to one or more sticks. First add the heavier things, such as pine cones, to get your mobile balanced. Then add lighter things, such as acorns. You can slide the yarn knots back and forth until your mobile balances. When you've got the strings in a position you like, use a little glue to hold them in place. Use another piece of yarn to hang up your mobile.

LEAF RUBBINGS

Place a leaf on a hard surface with the vein side up. Cover the leaf with a piece of paper. Remove the paper from a crayon (dark colors work best) and rub it horizontally over the leaf. If you have a clipboard, that's handy for keeping the paper in place. You can also try using chalk or colored pencils. Or bring your paper and crayons on a fall walk and make rubbings from tree bark.

ROASTED PUMPKIN SEEDS

Remove the seeds from a pumpkin and rinse them off. Dry the seeds with a clean kitchen towel. Preheat an oven to 300°F. Toss the seeds in 1 to 2 tablespoons of melted butter, olive oil, or margarine. Spread in a single layer on a baking sheet and sprinkle with salt. Bake, stirring seeds every 10 minutes. Bake 30 to 40 minutes until they start to brown. (Variations: hot—add cayenne pepper; tangy—add garlic salt and Worcestershire sauce; spiced—add cinnamon, ground ginger, and allspice.)

*Para mis amigos en Baires, dónde el otoño es primavera y
viceversa y estoy siempre confundido. Gracias por aguantarme.*

*(For my friends in Buenos Aires, where fall is spring and vice versa
and I'm always confused. Thanks for putting up with me.)*

—B. G.

Special thanks to Sally Doherty and April Ward for
their awesome creativity, encouragement, and patience;
and to Anna Franceschelli for the hand turkey.

Henry Holt and Company, LLC
Publishers since 1866
175 Fifth Avenue
New York, New York 10010
mackids.com

Henry Holt® is a registered trademark of Henry Holt and Company, LLC.
Copyright © 2012 by Bruce Goldstone
All rights reserved.

Library of Congress Cataloging-in-Publication Data
Goldstone, Bruce.
Awesome autumn / Bruce Goldstone. — 1st ed.
p.   cm.
ISBN 978-0-8050-9210-3 (hardcover)
1. Autumn—Juvenile literature. I. Title.
QB637.7.G65 2012   508.2—dc23   2011029043

First Edition—2012 / Designed by April Ward
Photo collages created with images from istockphoto.com and shutterstock.com.
Printed in China by Toppan Leefung Printing Ltd.,
Dongguan City, Guangdong Province

1 3 5 7 9 10 8 6 4 2

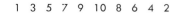